Minister's Manual For Baby Dedication

Minister's Manual For Baby Dedication

Unique and is relevant for such a time as this.
With declarations, prayers and pledges.
Desperate times calls for desperate measures!

Sandra J. Williams

XULON PRESS

Xulon Press
2301 Lucien Way #415
Maitland, FL 32751
407.339.4217
www.xulonpress.com

© 2023 by Sandy

All rights reserved solely by the author. The author guarantees all contents are original and do not infringe upon the legal rights of any other person or work. No part of this book may be reproduced in any form without the permission of the author.

Due to the changing nature of the Internet, if there are any web addresses, links, or URLs included in this manuscript, these may have been altered and may no longer be accessible. The views and opinions shared in this book belong solely to the author and do not necessarily reflect those of the publisher. The publisher therefore disclaims responsibility for the views or opinions expressed within the work.

Unless otherwise indicated, Scripture quotations taken from the Amplified Bible (AMP). Copyright © 1954, 1958, 1962, 1964, 1965, 1987 by The Lockman Foundation. Used by permission. All rights reserved. Scripture quotations taken from the New King James Version (NKJV). Copyright © 1982 by Thomas Nelson, Inc. Used by permission. All rights reserved.

Paperback ISBN-13: 9781662873263
Hard Cover ISBN-13: 9781662873270
Ebook ISBN-13: 9781662873287

Author's note

This baby dedication manual was inspired by the Spirit of God and is dedicated to Him. Its premise is to allow people to view the next generation and all those to follow as vitally important in the advancement of the kingdom of God.

Children ought to be regarded and embraced as a blessing and not a curse or an impediment; ask a woman who is barren! They are the most important work and not an obstruction from important work.

Table of Contents

Introduction – Each Child Matters to God 1
Minister's Statement of Encouragement 9
Decrees and Declarations of the Minister 11
Ministry to the Parent/s 13
Declarations/Pledges of the Parent/s 15
Declarations/Pledges of the Godparent/s 19
Prayer of Blessing and Dedication to the Lord 20
Prayer for Divine Directives, Direction,
and Provision 25
Conclusion–Guidelines for Parents 27

Introduction – Each Child Matters to God

The Word of the Lord spoken over a baby's/child's life has power to shape their life. Isaiah 55:10-11 (AMP) declares,

> *"For as the rain and snow come down from heaven, and do not return there without watering the earth, making it bear and sprout, and providing seed to the sower and bread to the eater, so will My word be which goes out of My mouth; it will not return to Me void (unless, without result), without accomplishing what I desire, and without succeeding in the matter for which I sent it."*

As a church and as ministers of the Gospel of Jesus Christ, we can no longer be nonchalant or passive as it pertains to children and their future. We have a divine responsibility to do what is humanly possible to preserve the lives and destinies of our children by allowing the supernatural abilities of God to flow through us unctioned by the Holy Ghost. By discerning the will of God as we minister in prayer. By laying on of hands making prophetic decrees over their lives with the expectation of the manifestation.

It is time for us to step up and take the initiative in our ministries against the assignment and the plots of the Enemy against the little ones by speaking the Word of God over them. The Word of the Lord is spirit and life (John 6:63). It transcends time, it is immutable, it is irrefutable, and it is settled in heaven forever (Psalm 119:89). Thus, it has the authority and the propensity to travel into their future and accomplish the divine purposes of God. The Word of the Lord can, in no way, return to Him void.

As ministers of the Gospel, we are likely to be the first prophet of the child's/children's destiny as we lay hands on them, speak, and pray prophetically over them. The Word of God coupled with prophetic prayer has the power to shape one's destiny. Timothy was encouraged by the Apostle Paul with these words: *"Do not neglect the gift that is in you,* **which was given to you by prophesy with the laying on of of the hands of the leadership"** (1 Timothy 4:14 NKJV) The law of contact, transmission, and impartation worked for Timothy, as seen in the Scripture. These same laws and principles worked for many others, and if applied, will continue to work for many others. All that is needed is the spark that will evidently ignite a fire.

We cannot underestimate the power of these laws. If the greeting Elizabeth received from Mary could have cause her baby (John the Baptist) to leap in her womb; and Elizabeth filled with the Holy Spirit (Luke 1:41), then why should we not believe that the power of God's spoken Word could cause blessings, and life to be made manifest? As carriers and conduits of the Spirit of Christ, why should we not believe we could prophesy the plans, purposes, and destiny of God in the lives of the children who we are dedicating to the Lord? Having the breath, the ruach and the life of God, we are positioned to function in the realm of faith to tap into His supernatural authority to call into being that which does not exist (Romans 4:17). Although not every minister has the prophetic or the seer mantle on their life, every Spirit-filled minister should prophesy (Acts 2:18b).

Each child matters to God and should be treated equally! Regardless of the spiritual, social, or economic status of the parent/s, each child should be presented to the Lord for dedication with the same enthusiasm, seeing them through the lens of the Spirit having divine purpose and destiny assigned to their lives. It should not be about whose child we are presenting to the Lord for dedication. It could be the child of a prophet, an evangelist, or an unbeliever. No matter where they come from, they all belong to God our Father.

The threshold of the great awakening and end time revival that is yet to be seen is going to take place not only through the remnant who has not defiled themselves, but also through children. One of the examples in Scriptures that proves that children are not exempt from God's kingdom agenda is recorded in the Gospel according to the Book of Matthew. The children were crying out in the temple and saying, "Hosanna to the Son of David!" And when the chief priests and the scribes (the religious leaders) became upset and presumptuously asked Jesus if He heard what the children were saying, Jesus replied, "Yes," as He affirmed their involvement in worship. He further challenged the knowledge of the chief priests' and the scribes' with biblical references to what the children were doing. Jesus asked, "Have you never read, out of the mouth of babes and nursing infants you have perfected praise?" (Matthew 21:15-16 NKJV). The Old Testament Scripture also establish evidence that children are included in God's kingdom agenda. "Josiah was eight years old when he became king..." (2 Kings 22:1 NKJV).

Scripture reveals that, *From the days of John the Baptist until now the kingdom of heaven suffers violent assault, and violent men seize it by force [as a precious prize]* (Matthew 11:12 AMP). Biblical history also reveals that the plan of the Enemy was always to destroy the male seed (Exodus 1:22; Matthew 2:16-18). They were more prone to the onslaught of the Enemy; it is no different in this era. The Pharaohs and the Herods of today still hold fast to the same nefarious agenda. The only difference today is that there is no gender disparity; the plot is inclusive of the male and the female gender.

The rate of suicide among children and adolescents is either an under-emphasized or a concealed epidemic. God's precious children are made to believe that the only way out of whatever they are experiencing is to end their lives; thus, aborting their divine purpose and destiny. If this is not an assignment from the council of hell, then I do not know what is.

I believe that ministers should become proactive and place more emphasis on the importance of baby dedication. We can no longer gloss over and make light of such services, otherwise we will lose the battle over their lives. More often than not, baby dedication services are cut short so that we can get on with the rest of what we believe is the "meat" of the day's gathering, but I believe it is time to change that concept and become more deliberate, even if it means scheduling it for a separate time of day. When we look at young ones being presented to the Lord for dedication, we may think that the fulfillment of their God-ordained purposes is too farfetched to be considered, but it is needful to be reminded that we all were chosen by God before the foundation of the world (Ephesians 1:4). When we consider this truth, there is absolutely no reason for us to even entertain the thought that their lives should not be counted as vitally important in kingdom advancement. Before long, it becomes their time; they will become our successors in the advancement of the kingdom of God before any of us know it.

I am aware that God has deposited parental abilities in each adult and some learn the heart of parenting progressively, but I believe the spiritual aspect of parenting must be taught and learned from the Holy Scriptures. Not everyone knows of the ill-effect that can proceed from their spoken words and actions toward a child. Therefore, I believe that this manual can initiate and motivate some changes in the way people view the lives of our little ones. I believe we can utilize the opportunity to make a deposit that can and will impact the parent/s as they listen and are directed to make the decrees and declarations (Job 22:28), and grasp the concept and the importance of what we are trying to initiate and implement.

In doing this, I have the faith to believe that this would have a lasting impact on not only the child/children, but also on the parent/s when they see how much emphasis is placed on baby dedication and become deeply rooted in the fundamentals. My desire and, hopefully, the desire of every minister is to see the plans of God being executed in the life of children. For it is written in the Gospel according to John 10:10 (AMP) that, *"The thief comes only in order to steal and kill and destroy. I came that they may have life, and have it in abundance [to the full, till it overflows]."* The Enemy consequently shows no partiality in his plots to annihilate.

As Jesus treasures children, so should the church and its ministers. There littleness does not diminish their predetermined purpose from God on Earth. Although Timothy was not a baby, but a teenager, the Apostle Paul told Timothy that he should not allow anyone to despise his youth. He was encouraged to embrace his calling. (1 Timothy 4:12-16)

It is my firm belief, as I was directed by the Lord to pen this manual, that the use of it will have an eternal impact on children and their parents. The session of dedicating their children to the Lord will initiate a response to continue to do as they will be directed to enhance their eternal destiny.

Minister's Statement of Encouragement

As a minister of the Gospel of Jesus Christ, I acknowledge and believe that *Children are a heritage from the Lord, the fruit of the womb is a reward* (Psalm 127:3 NKJV).

Our Lord places a very high value on humanity and children are in no way exempt. In the Gospel according to Mark chapter 10, while people were bringing children to Jesus that He might touch them, the disciples rebuked them. Jesus was angry because of their choice of action and adamantly told His disciples, *"Let the little children come to Me, and do not forbid them; for of such is the kingdom of God"* (Mark 10:14 NJKV).

The significance of this service cannot be overemphasized. Jesus implemented, "Let the little children come to Me!" Children are not a biological accident, neither are they test tube trials. They are created in the image and likeness of our Lord. They are intricately and intrinsically designed and blueprinted according to and for God's will and purpose. It could be that we are dedicating to the Lord today, the next apostle, prophet, evangelist, pastor, or teacher, the next president/prime minister who will be a trailblazing change agent for God's glory. Unless the Lord reveals such things, we just never know. Therefore, we do not take this God-ordained opportunity lightly.

Your decision to bring your little one/s to be presented to the Lord is an indication that you are acknowledging that you need the Lord's help and divine intervention in raising your child/children. You are seeking His touch and His blessings upon the life of your child/children. For, *Unless the Lord builds the house, they labor in vain who builds it; unless the Lord guards the city, the watchman keeps awake in vain* (Psalm 127:1 NKJV).

It is not incidental that you are standing before these witnesses to present your child/children to the Lord. It is by divine order. The part that you played was being obedient in bringing your child/children to the house of the Lord.

What I am about to share as a minister of the Lord, has the propensity to invoke the will, plans, and purposes of God in the life of your child/children. It will also help to navigate his/her life as I use the Word of God and invite Him to be his/her/their Divine GPS who will lead, and guide him/her/them into his/her/their God-ordained purpose and destiny.

Decrees and Declarations of the Minister

Today, we are privileged to dedicate a child/children to their Heavenly Father! The minister will begin the dedication of the child/children with the following declarations, filling in the blanks with the child's/children's name/s:

1) I decree and declare that (_____) was born for a purpose and with a purpose.

2) I decree and declare that the Lord formed (_____)'s inward parts, and covered him/her/them in his/her/their mother's womb (Psalm 139:13).

3) I decree and declare that God saw (_____)'s substance before he/she/they was/were formed, and in His eternal Book, his/her/their days were all written. (Psalm 139:16) Therefore, God has a preordained plan, purpose, and destiny for (_____)'s life.

4) I decree and declare that every God-ordained plan, purpose, and destiny for (_____) will come to full fruition and be made manifest without restraint or interruption!

5) I decree and declare that (_____) shall be a joy and delight to his/her/their parent/s!

Ministry to the Parents

With the purpose for the child/children declared, the time has come to counsel the parent/s. Address fathers and mothers by name; make them feel as much a part of this dedication as their child/children for they are performing an incredible act for their child/children. Read the following scriptures and interact with the parent/s as follows, filling in the blanks with the parent/s name/s:

1) *He who withholds the rod [of discipline] hates his son [daughter], but who loves him [her] disciplines and trains him [her] diligently and appropriately [with wisdom and love.* Proverbs 13:24 (AMP)

(_____), as a parent/s, it is your responsibility to use the Scriptures and not the dictates of the systems of the world as your guide in raising your child/children. If you agree to utilize scriptural discipline, say, **"I/we agree."**

2) *And you, fathers, do not provoke your children to anger [do not exasperate them to the point of resentment with demands that are trivial or unreasonable or humiliating or abusive; nor showing*

favoritism or indifference to any of them], bring them up [tenderly, with lovingkindness] in the discipline and instruction of the Lord. Ephesians 6:4 (AMP)

(_____), if you agree not to provoke your child/children to wrath, but to bring him/her them up tenderly with lovingkindness in the disciple and instruction of the Lord, say, **"I agree."**

3) *Death and life are in the power of the tongue.* Proverbs 18:21 (AMP).

(_____), the formative years of a child's life are not to be taken lightly or disregarded. Therefore, it is vital that you use your tongue wisely when you speak to them, about them, and over them (whether in their presence or in their absence). In other words, speak life; speak words of faith and affirmation which will help to build and develop their confidence, self-respect, and self-esteem that will ultimately help to shape their destiny. If you agree to speak words of life and affirmation and not death over the life of your child/children, say, **"I/we agree."**

Declarations/Pledges of the Parent/s

The parent/s are to repeat after the minister the following acknowledgements and pledges. Blank spaces are to be filled with the child's/children's name/s.

"**(Name/s of parent/s), before God and all of these witnesses:**"

1) I/We acknowledge that (_____) is/are God's gift/s to me/us. Therefore, I/we commit to cherish this/these gift/s from the Lord.

2) I/We pledge not to physically, verbally, or emotionally abuse (_____).

3) I/We pledge not to allow tangible things to replace spending time with (_____).

4) I/We pledge not to allow television or social media to raise (_____).

5) I/We pledge to love, encourage, and most importantly, pray for (_____).

6) I/We pledge to correct and instruct (_____) in a loving manner.

7) I/We pledge to express my/our love to (_____), my/our God-given gift with my/our words and deeds.

8) I/We pledge to partner with God in the development of (_____)'s spiritual, emotional, psychological, physical, scholastic, and social wellbeing.

9) I/We pledge to partner with the church as I/we will with the school by bringing (_____) to the house of the Lord, for this may be their first, but it will in no way be their last.

10) I/We acknowledge that God has made us all uniquely different. Different people have different gifts, talents, and innate abilities. We were not created to fit in the same mold. Therefore, I/we will not impose my/our own desires upon (_____) because his/her/their divine calling, purpose, and career path are unique and God-ordained. He/She/They is/are unique to his/her/their personality, and I/

we will help to guide him/her/them toward his/her/their strategically predestined bent!

11) My/Our child's/children's uniqueness was ordained by God. Therefore, I will not compare (_____) to any sibling or to anyone else. I will not show favoritism. I will not be indifferent, but I will love (_____) equally in spite of his/her/their differences in personality and achievements!

Declarations/Pledges of the Godparent/s

While not as common nowadays, parents may still wish to bless their child/children with godparents. Whether one godparent or both is chosen, they are also an important part of a baby dedication. The godparents are to repeat after the minister the following acknowledges and pledges filling in the blanks with the name/s of the godchild/godchildren.

"**(Name/s of godparent/s), before God and all of these witnesses:**"

1) As a godparent, my/our responsibility is to aid the parent/s in raising (_____). I/We commit to help in supporting (_____) in every way possible and in all ways necessary according to my/our abilities.

2) I/We pledge to be a blessing to (_____) in tangible ways, and be involved in his/her life spiritually, financially, physically, and emotionally.

Prayer of Blessing and Dedication to the Lord

Heavenly Father, hallowed be Your name! Let Your kingdom come and let Your will be done in this child's/these children's life just as it is in heaven, whom You have predetermined to be born and to be here today, even before the foundation of the world. Father, we acknowledge that You have a strategic plan, purpose, and divine destiny for this child/these children. Therefore, I ask that You let them come to full fruition and be made manifest. Father, give this child/these children the ability to hear Your voice like Samuel; give him/her/them the ability to discern and decipher Your will from the Enemy's, and grace them with the tenacity to choose Your will and Your path. Let Your divine will become his/her/their reality.

Father, our dependence is upon You for everything concerning the life of this child/these children. Apart from You, we can do nothing, for it is not by might nor by power, but by Your Spirit, oh Lord of Hosts. Put the seal of Your Spirit upon (_____) from this day forward. Father, place Your indelible mark upon his/her/their life, and like

Moses desired to suffer affliction with the people of God, rather than endure the pleasures of sin for a season, let it also be the choice of this child/these children when they become of age. Cause him/her/them to be a joy and delight to his/her/their parents. Let honoring his/her/their parents be constant, so that it will be well with him/her/them and longevity will be his/her/their portion.

Let every plot of the Enemy against his/her/their life be foiled in Jesus's name and let not the Enemy have dominion in or over any area of (_____)'s life. I declare that this child/these children shall know who he is/she is/they are. There shall be no identity nor gender confusion. There shall be no sexual, physical, or emotional abuse imposed upon (_____)'s life. There shall be no incestuous relations. There shall be no substance abuse. There shall be no premature nor untimely death, whether by suicide, murder, incidents, or accidents, in Jesus's name! (_____) shall live and not die, and declare the works of the Lord. I decree and declare that no evil shall befall (_____), neither shall any plague go near his/her/their dwelling place. I decree and declare that no generational curse shall manifest in his/her/their life. Lord, let none of Your plans for this child/these children be annihilated.

Father, when (_____) comes of age, cause him/her/them to be a great godly leader/s and not a follower/s. Give him/her/them the grace to choose his/her/their friends and associates wisely. Cause him/her/them to become conduits of Your power and change agents in all of his/

her/their spheres of influence for Your glory and for Your honor. I decree and declare that (_____) shall use his/her/their God-given gifts to glorify the name of the Lord. I decree and declare that (_____) shall fulfill his/her/their kingdom assignments. Father, bless his/her/their going out and coming in from this time forth and forevermore. Lord, I present (_____) to You and I decree and declare that he/she is/they are blessed and dedicated to You for life.

In the name of the Father and of the Son and of the Holy Ghost. Amen!

Prayer for Divine Directives, Direction, and Provision

Heavenly Father, it is You who has chosen the parents of this child/these children, and today, I present him/her/them to You. Father, grant to them great grace that they will never neglect this child/these children. May You grant to them the grace, patience, and wisdom to train up (_____) in the way he/she/they should go, so that when he/she is/they are old, he/she/they will not depart from it. Cause them to see the imperativeness of the spiritual aspect of their child's/children's life.

I pray that they will make daily deposits of Your Word in the hearing and in the hearts of this child/these children. Cause them to never cease to speak words of affirmation to their child/children. Cause them to pray ceaselessly and give them the urge to bring their child/children weekly into Your sanctuary. Grant to them everything that is needed for their wellbeing, and the wellbeing of (_____) so that there will be no lack in their lives because You are El Shaddai, the All-Sufficient One.

Father, give these parents the divine ability to discern the right babysitter/s so that there will be no abuse, neglect, nor negative influence imposed upon the life of this child/these children. Father, by Your will, cause them to discern the right schools and cause them to be above and not beneath. May You give them divine direction (if not this church) to a Bible teaching, Spirit-filled church. Heavenly Father, we agree in prayer, and we thank You for prayers answered.

In Jesus's name. Amen!

Conclusion—Guidelines for Parents

Although most parent/s see the need to dedicate their little one/s to the Lord, not all are born-again believers, so speaking the Word of the Lord and making declarations over the child's/children's life may be the first and, sadly, the last. Therefore, declaration of the Word of God and prophetic praying as we receive insight and foresight from the Spirit of the Lord are equally imperative if we are going to see a turnaround in the lives and destiny of children.

Parents, God has undoubtedly entrusted you with one of the greatest responsibilities, and if you will take heed to His principles, you will do great justice and due diligence to your child/children. In order for your child/children not to become mere statistics or a liability to society, let him/her/them be an asset and a positive change agent for God's glory.

Be your child's/children's greatest influencer and encourager, otherwise someone else, or the painful reality of the ever-changing persuasive culture of demonic influences will. Children live what they learn. If you teach your child/children truth at an early age this will cause him/her to have a profound discerning awareness whenever lies are perpetrated.

Present the Lord Jesus to your child/children as soon as he/she/they display the ability to comprehend the Gospel. Raise up your child/children in the fear of the Lord. Let him/her/them know that He created, loves, desires to have a relationship with, and has the greatest plan for his/her/their life. Let your child/children be involved in your daily praying and Bible reading and allow him/her/them to share his/her/their understanding of it.

The experiences with each may differ. Regardless of any of his/her/their actions or reactions, refrain from casting judgement. May you always be aware that there is innate divine potential in him/her/them.

Lastly, spend quality time with your child/children. This will cause you to know if/when something is off. Build trust; children need someone to confide in, let that person/s be you. Give your child/children your ears when necessary. Be involved.